PHUKET

Fiona Nichols

TIMES EDITIONS

Phuket
Times Editions
422 Thomson Road, Singapore 1129.

Typeset by Superskill, Singapore.
Printing and colour separation
by Tien Wah Press, Singapore.

ISBN: 9971-40-017-0

Contents

Phuket was very much on the map long before this wiry old tin miner posed for his portrait, above, in the late 19th century. Its trading importance was well-established by the time Denis, d'apres Mannevillette, drew the island marked "Junkseilon", right, and its neighbouring coastline for an hydrographic atlas published in 1745.

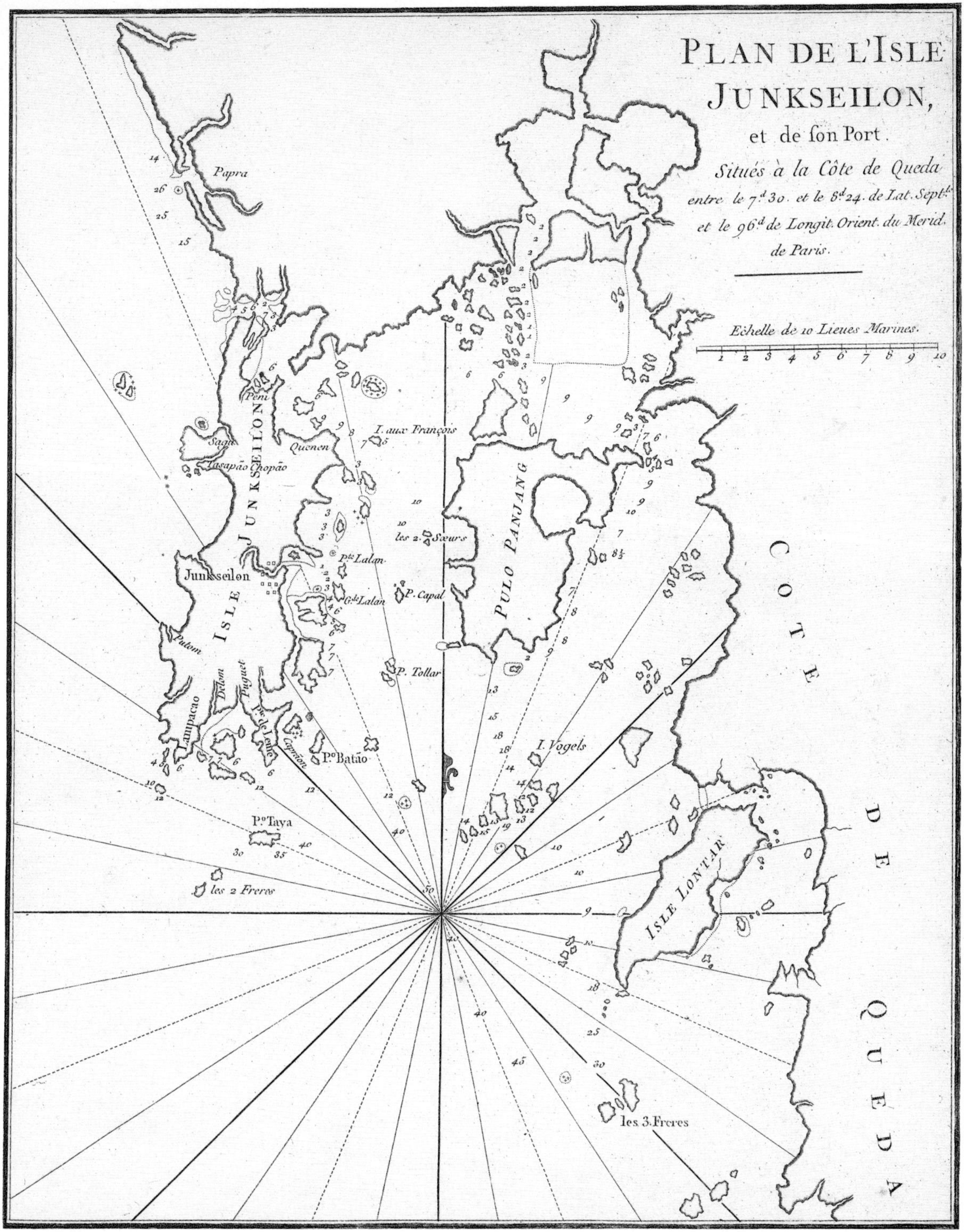

PLAN DE L'ISLE JUNKSEILON,
et de son Port.
Situés à la Côte de Queda
entre le 7.d 30. et le 8d 24. de Lat. Septle.
et le 96d de Longit. Orient. du Merid. de Paris.
Echelle de 10 Lieues Marines.
1 2 3 4 5 6 7 8 9 10
Papra
Peni
Saga
Tasapão
Chopão
Quenen
I. aux François
ISLE JUNKSEILON
Junkseilon
Pte. Lalan
Gde. Lalan
P. Capal
les 2 Sœurs
PULO PANJANG
Putom
Delom
Puguet
Pte. de Lente
Lampacao
Caprion
P. Tollar
Po. Batão
Po. Taya
les 2 Freres
I. Vogels
ISLE LONTAR
les 3 Freres
COTE DE QUEDA

The Pearl Opens

They say that flawless pearls portend fortune and in the case of Phuket Island, in southern Thailand, this old adage holds true. The fortunes were not just the traditional ones of minerals, amber or indeed the natural sea pearls found offshore, but those associated with that modern-day jewel, tourism. For this island — known as the "Pearl of the South" – had for decades remained a secret holiday hideaway of wealthy Thais, until its "discovery" in the mid Seventies by sunseeking travellers of the world.

Graced by some 16 fine, pristine, sandy beaches, swathed in thick tropical vegetation, blessed by an equable warm climate and populated by the gentle Thais, Phuket has finally been placed firmly on the tourist map. Although its commercial importance was recognised centuries ago by both greedy invaders and the government of Thailand, it had to wait until the 1970's for the realisation of its true potential.

As the aircraft banks to land at Phuket's international airport, the island's prime attractions are visible to the visitor whose enchanted gaze sweeps over the panoramic vistas of crystal clear, blue ocean, verdant foliage and pearly white beaches. It is a seductive patchwork of colour which foretells the harmonious pattern of life below. Nature is bountiful and the inhabitants are at peace.

Located some 931 kms. south of Bangkok, the capital of Thailand, the island of Phuket lies on the westerly seaboard washed by the warm waters of the Andaman Sea, a few hundred kilometres north of Malaysia's Langkawi and Penang islands. Stretching from its northern tip to the southern shores, Phuket is 48·7 kms. long and 21·3 kms. wide and joined at the far north to the mainland by Sarasin Bridge.

In the centre of the island lies a hilly granite backbone which is increasingly being cleared for agriculture, but pockets of primary jungle still remain in parts of the west coast and in the Khao Phra Thaeo National Park — vegetation that has changed little since the early Europeans discovered this strategic island over three centuries ago.

In those tranquil moments around dawn and dusk, when the air is stilled, the magic of Phuket reveals itself. Maybe a solitary fisherman will cross the magenta sunset or perhaps the lingering rays hold the sun's warmth long after setting, giving an ethereal – even psychedelic – quality to the panorama. Phuket is an ever-changing pageant of colours and silhouettes.

From the air Phuket's central granite backbone snakes towards the blue horizon of mainland Thailand, below. One approach route brings passengers in over mangrove swamps – a wild, sparsely inhabited area – whilst the other sweeps down over the island's sandy beaches. The limestone stack dominating Phi Phi Island's northern sandy shores, right, is as impressive as its better-known peer in Phang Nga Bay. Framed by feathery palms and the translucent, pure hues of crystalline waters, this is a favourite point for many visitors to pause and drink in the scene. Overleaf: The fantasyland of towering limestone cliffs at Phang Nga Bay loom over a lone fisherman from Pannyi, returning home in the lingering glow of the setting sun.

Phuket is Thailand's largest island, and for the purposes of administration the only one to be made an entire province out of the 73 provincial districts.

Yet even in this relatively small island — nearly 600 sq. km. in total — there are numerous natural attractions. The geological formation of Phuket and its surrounding islands is quite breathtaking for the millenia have taken their toll on the limestone and granite land, which once formed a continuous mass, creating a series of stacks, grottos and islands with sheer rock faces.

From the air nearby Phang Nga Bay is a marvel dotted with isolated shapes; from sea-level it is a wonderland of grotesque, unique and totally fascinating rocky forms.

The island of Phuket boasts two waterfalls — the source of drinking water for many villages either side of the escarpment — and a western shoreline that is the Utopia of tourists and visitors from the north.

Trade and Tributes

That indefatigable Egyptian traveller, Ptolemy, was probably one of the first adventurers in history to visit the island of Phuket. That he found what are nowadays called Malaysia, Burma and Thailand in the first century A.D. is certain, for he drew up a map under the name of the Golden Khersonese which outlined this elongated peninsula and marked some of the offshore islands. Of course, it was not wildly accurate, nor was Phuket specifically mentioned, but it was the first attempt at cartography for this area. Then, until the 16th century and the arrival of European navigators, there is a scarcity of historical documentation.

The earliest settlers on the island are believed to have migrated via the Andaman Seas from the Mon Khmer region of Pegu, now in Burma. They chose to put down roots in the northern half of what we now call Phuket Island. In addition came another group — probably from Indonesia — of nomadic people, called in Thai *Chao Ley* or *Chao Nam*, sea or water people, whose unique gypsy-like lifestyle is paralleled by others of similar stock in Burma and Thailand. These folk still inhabit certain coastal areas and offshore islands.

Yet, despite numerous erudite attempts, no one has been able to offer a definitive explanation of the origins of the Phuketians; much remains speculation.

In those distant days the island of Phuket was not known by its present name and nor did the early travellers realise it was in fact an island, separated from the general land mass. Until colonial times it was believed to be a peninsula jutting out from the Siamese mainland. It was known as "Junk Ceylon" or even "Iunsalan" depending on who was pronouncing and who was writing the name. In this epoch the island was already divided into three distincts: Thalang, Kathu and Phuket.

Early travellers mention the copious deposits of tin on the island and comment on the ambergris, wood supplies, amber and rhino horn that the natives willingly traded. The calm, safe waters off the east coast soon became a favourite stopping point for seafarers who would pause on their journeys for fresh

The island's two 18th century heroines are immortalised forever in bronze, above, at Tha Rua crossroads on the route from Phuket Airport to town. Honoured by the locals for their valiant defence of Tha Rua against the Burmese, the sisters Chan and Muk are often swathed in sashes of honour or traditional Thai dress.
Fine old mansions are faded monuments to Phuket's mining riches and, like the one on Krabi Road, photographed left, stand peacefully in sprawling grounds.

Although Thailand was never colonised like her neighbours, Europe influenced the rich. When Governor Korsimbi posed for his official portrait, above, early this century he wore braided regalia befitting his role as the man who helped put Phuket on the world map.

For wedding portraits the Chinese preferred elaborate costumes imported from China. Since the community was small, wives were sought in neighbouring Straits Chinese settlements and the bride of the scion of a wealthy family, photographed right, came from Penang.

supplies and water. By the 17th century the island became one of the eight tributary kingdoms of the Siamese capital, Ayutthaya, and its wealth was siphoned by royal monopoly. Despite this, a few Europeans were granted licences to trade with the locals — and this they did profitably.

Once Phuket's strategic location and abundant wealth were noted by the Europeans struggling for supremacy in Asia, the race was on to colonise the island. The French sallied forth; the Portuguese set up religious missions; the Dutch had designs on it and the English made exploratory trips. Francis Light, English trader and sometime-envoy, married a local girl and began doing business in Phuket, leaving it in 1786 in favour of Penang. Whether it was the threat of invasion, or the British panic to secure a settlement in the face of potential Dutch domination of trading routes, is not certain, but Penang was the choice. Had Light and the British not made the decision, Phuket might well have been part of the later British Empire.

In 1785 the threat of invasion became a reality to the inhabitants of Phuket as the belligerent Burmese began the first of their three main invasions. During the first five-week insurgence two young sisters rose to fame and became national heroines.

The governor of the northern town of Thalang had just died. His courageous widow, Chan, along with her sister Muk, assumed responsibility for the town's defence. Thao Thep Kasattri and her sister, Thao Si Sunthorn, (as they were later entitled by King Rama I) saved the town of Thalang in a valiant defence by grouping the inhabitants in a fortified area, and disguising the womenfolk as male soldiers in a crafty bid to outwit the Burmese. They succeeded and were duly honoured for their role.

Today their statues stand south of Thalang town, on the road between Phuket town and the airport and, more often than not, islanders decorate them with garlands of flowers in appreciation of the sisters' deeds. It was from this event that the modern history of Phuket dates.

It took two more invasions by the Burmese until the peace-loving islanders were able to settle in the beginning of the 19th century. Then came a wave of

Chinese immigrants, lured by the lucrative tin deposits from which the great Sino-Thai dynasties in Phuket made their names. Malays, too, migrated into southern Thailand and arrived in Phuket, swelling the population. It was a continuous wave of prosperity for some and for others — who ultimately rebelled against their strict Chinese overlords — a life of relentless toil. Chinese arbitrators were finally sent from the homeland to quell the unrest and peace was again restored.

The beginning of the 20th century was a period of positive growth for the islanders as tin mining boomed, the benevolent local governor, Korsimbi, developed the island's economy and the capital, Phuket, began its modern expansion. King Rama V urged expatriated Phuketians, who had fled the island during the Burmese sacking, to return from Krabi and Phang Nga provinces and settle themselves anew in Phuket. In 1907 an Australian, Captain Edward Thomas Miles, introduced the first tin dredger to the island which

The manager and staff of Phuket Golf Club pose at the turn of the century in the grounds of the clubhouse at Surin. White tropical jackets and solar topees were standard uniform of the era.

opened up a vast and hitherto untouched area for mineral recovery.

In 1933 the island officially became the Province of Phuket under the administration of the central Thai government which successively allocates a governor for three-year terms of rule.

As the world demand for tin took a dip in the middle of this century a new industry emerged in Phuket to replenish the local coffers. At first tentative, tourism began to make its mark in the Seventies and now accounts for revenues exceeding a billion baht annually. On this wave of success, even small-time traders have ridden along, starting ice-cream parlours and snack bars in some of the most unlikely spots. The small national airport is now an international one with nearly a hundred weekly flights.

In their gentle, friendly way Phuketians have embraced newcomers and adapted their lives to include the foreigners who flock to their sunny shores.

The menfolk of a Chinese clan pose before a row of handsome terrace houses showing European and traditional Chinese influences in their elaborate architecture.

The Melting Pot

Today it's sometimes hard to tell a Thai from a Chinese or Malay when you first visit Phuket. Chinese and Thai have intermarried: both are predominantly Buddhist yet have very different temples for worship; some have even been converted by Christian missionaries whose presence is still felt in Phuket. The darker skinned Thais often look similar to those Malays who have migrated to the island yet retained their Muslim way of life. The only groups which have any homogeneity are the largely Animist *Chao Ley* or Sea Gypsies and the obvious expatriates, be they European or Indian. Phuketians are a result of a huge racial and religious melting pot.

The Thai way of life is intrinsically a Buddhist way of life, yet in Phuket Muslims, Buddhists, Sikhs, Christians and Animists live side by side without tension and follow a very similar lifestyle.

When the first Europeans landed 300 years ago, the dark-skinned natives of Phuket were the so-called Thais who had previously migrated from the area we now call Burma. They inhabited the northern districts — Kathu and Thalang — and were an agrarian people. Things have changed little today.

The gentle natured Thais tend to be rural dwellers, preferring the less hurried pace of life and leaving the urban settlement to their Chinese brethren. Like rural Thais elsewhere in the kingdom, they prefer the casual and practical sartorial style of the Thai sarong; bright flowery patterns for the females and checked material for the males.

In harmony with nature, Thais live in attractive homes built on stilts among the plantations or, if they are seafaring, along the seashore. Homes are sparse and immaculate; cleanliness is very important to a good Buddhist. Usually constructed of wood and traditionally thatched with *nipa* palm (now, all too frequently corrugated iron, that bane of the Third World, is used for roofing), Thai homes stand above a beaten ground courtyard which serves as garden, play area and sometime work place.

The Thai religious temple, the *wat*, plays an impor-

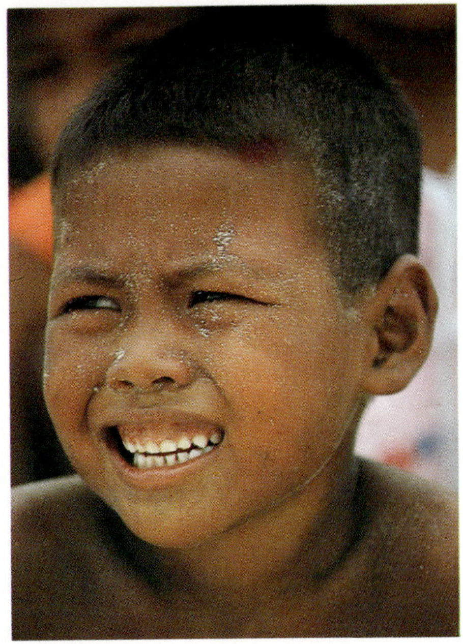

Tradition dies hard for young and old alike: although the Malaysian-born Chinese grandmother, left, has lived in Phuket Town for the greater part of her life, she still prefers her native Hokkien dialect to Thai. And the young Chao Ley boy, above, like most Sea Gypsies, speaks only his community's dialect.

tant part in a Thai's life. Although it is not necessary to visit it regularly, as with some other faiths, it provides a spiritual "safe house" — somewhere that is open to all people at all times — for quiet reflection and meditation. Senior monks provide encouragement and instruct those who seek advice but generally the Buddhist religion is taught to the young through parental and scholastic guidance.

At some time in each diligent male Thai Buddhist's life, he retreats to the *wat* for anything from a week to six months to learn and meditate, study the scriptures and adopt the austere habits of the permanent monks — a useful and self-instructive period. As with his full-time peers, he will rise long before dawn and set off at first light carrying the traditional round alms bowl to collect food, for a Buddhist monk may not cook and does not buy his victuals. Even today the saffron-robed monk, with his closely shaven head, is a familiar sight in Thailand clasping his dark earthenware pot as he

East and West cohabit colourfully in Thailand: cursive Thai writing adds an exotic touch to internationally familiar products, below, and the Thai bride posing left wears all the finery of a Western wedding – but only after bowing to the time-honoured Asian tradition of choosing an auspicious day for the ceremony.

Pressed and pristine schoolchildren line up before the morning's lessons, their faces daubed with a chalky paste which protects and cools the skin.

waits, eyes cast down, outside homes, shops or hotels for an offering. Times may change, but Buddhist basics do not.

From outside, a Thai *wat* is a glittering, highly decorated symbol of the faith while inside all such trappings are ignored in favour of a clean simplicity conducive to peaceful thought. Except for images of the Buddha, the interior is unadorned.

Of the 29 *wats* in Phuket, two have a special place for the islanders. The first, Wat Pra Tong (a couple of kilometres north of Thalang), was built on a spot, according to legend, where a young boy, charged with caring for the water buffalo, had tethered a beast to a metal-like stick rising from the ground. The child fell ill and died but his father had a dream which led him back to the spot where his son had tied down the animal. He, too, found the stick and began to dig, uncovering a solid gold image of Buddha. Despite much effort, they were unable to free the whole statue and so built a *wat* around the half image. Years later the invading Burmese tried to remove the valuable statue but were also unable to dig it out. Once they had retreated the villagers decided to cover the image with plaster so that it would no longer instil such greed. Today the bust remains, covered with fragile slips of gold leaf which are lovingly pressed onto the statue in the Buddhist custom.

The second, and better known, temple is Wat Chalong where there are enshrined the likenesses of Luang Pho Chaem and Luang Po Chaung, two of the island's most respected monks. History relates that in 1876, during the short uprising by Chinese immigrants labouring in the tin mines, it was Luang Pho Chaem aided by his fellow brother, who rallied the people and managed to quell the rebellion. For his deed he was elevated to the rank of Phra Khru Wisutthiowong-sachan — a great distinction. Nowadays Thais flock to the temple and decorate the images of the two famous monks with gold leaf, lighting incense to their memory.

The Thais in Phuket celebrate a number of national holidays: there is *Songkran*, the old Thai New Year, when water is thrown over everyone in a mischievous mood of fun marking the end of the old year; *Loy Krathong* (Festival of Lights) which is a moving visual

spectacle where small "boats" are set sail on water during the hours of darkness carrying the fragile, flickering flame of a small oil candle and *Maka Puja* when more candlelight processions are held around Buddhist temples.

In addition to this there is the unique Phuketian Vegetarian Festival. This is ten days of strict vegetarianism and accompanying meditation in order to cleanse the body and soul. Participants will then go into a trance and pierce their bodies with hooks and spikes, leaving little apparent after effect. For Phuket this is the major annual festival where dancing, music and itinerant vendors are all part of the fun.

The first Chinese arrived in Thailand some 600 years ago after the Mongols invaded their own country but it was only 150 years ago that they began to settle in Phuket. They came, not from the capital but from the south — Penang, Malaysia and Singapore — enticed by the stories of mineral riches. In 1897 the census counted

Buddhism is Thailand's national religion and its architecture and rituals leave a strong imprint on the daily way of life. The country's glittering, golden image is constantly reinforced by slithers of gold leaf being pressed on statues of the Buddha, below, housed in magnificent temples like the newly-built Wat Tha Rua, below right. Early each morning, monks silently walk the streets gathering offerings of food, flowers and basic necessities from the faithful whose gift-giving gains them merit. Overleaf: The bric-a-brac of a traditional Chinese craftsman's shop. Light from the street illuminates this jeweller's bench and the wall of family portraits beside him.

9 10 11 12 13 14
16 17 18 19 20 21
Ko-Yo
Latex

Wherever they settle in the world, the Chinese always keep their traditions alive. During Phuket's annual ten-day Vegetarian Festival Chinese mediums go into trance, right, and skewer their bodies before taking part in street processions accompanied by gongs and firecrackers, below. Noise is an essential part of Chinese funerals, too, as professional musicians accompany the gaudy hearse and sackcloth-covered mourners, below right, in deafening cacophany.

11,350 Chinese coolies (working in the tin mines), comprising 40 percent of the population. Nowadays the figure is nearer 30 percent but the Chinese community is still a strong unit and one which has more ties with its southern neighbours than its northern peers. Many Chinese inhabitants of Phuket still speak their Hokkien dialect and have family or cousins in Malaysia.

Predominantly businessmen, the Sino-Thais favour urban dwelling and account for nearly half the town's population. It was the Chinese overlords who put tin mining on the map and they who developed the industry. In consequence, practically all the lovely old colonial homes are owned by Sino-Thai families who have adopted the ways of their new homeland but still retain many of the traditions and foibles of their own culture. With the changing nature of business in Phuket, some smart Sino-Thais have wound down their interests in the waning tin and rubber industries and turned to the tourist trade. Many hotels, shops and

restaurants are owned by Chinese families.

Scattered all over the island are the brightly-coloured Chinese temples, varying in size. Like their Thai counterparts they are refuges, but far more elaborately decorated both internally and externally. As Thais light the heavily-scented incense sticks and pray in front of an image of Buddha, so the Chinese do similarly to a number of Taoist deities who have different protective roles.

Chinese New Year is the big festival in the Sino-Thai's calendar; a time when families traditionally reunite and the ancestors are remembered with a lavish feast of food offerings. The private family altars are decorated and venerated by all before the Chinese family, as always pragmatic, sit down and eat the feast. Because the Sino-Thais form a minority community in Thailand, this festival is not such a big affair as it is in more Chinese-dominated countries.

Thai Muslims account for some 25 percent of the

Splendid carving and gilding decorate the double doors, windows and air vents of a traditional Chinese home, below, on Thanon Yaowaraj – testimony to the entrepreneurial riches earned in Phuket early this century. The three interior photographs, right, show the eclectic mixture of decorations in a prominent Sino-Thai's ancestral home – European, Chinese and Thai.

population and tend to keep their lives very much to themselves. Originally they migrated from Malaysia and southern Thailand and settled on the shores of Phuket where they still dwell today. The areas around Sapum, Chalong Bay and Surin are all favoured by Muslim communities. Although some work in the rubber plantations in western Thailand, and a few more live in town, most choose the simple life of fishing folk and keep to their communities scattered along the shore.

Visitors to Phuket enjoy visiting the Muslims on Ko Pannyi, Phang Nga Bay who perch in their stilted wooden homes, high above the waters of the bay. They lead a comfortable life fishing the abundant supplies from this bay and either selling their catch to the local market in Phang Nga town or producing fish bi-products such as pastes and dried additives for Thai cuisine. Despite their somewhat cramped lifestyle, their homes and "streets" are clean and neat, in fact

The Muslim mosque at Surin, below, is the largest on Phuket and every Friday the faithful gather to pray and then join friends outside to eat at vendors' stalls and wander in the colourful local market. Day after day this venerable Muslim man, right, sits under the shady trees surrounding his home at Bang Thao – a predominantly Muslim village near Surin Mosque. His wife sits companionably beside him, passing the time of day and tending to his needs.

somewhat more so than those of many of their fellow dwellers on *terra firma*.

The goals of a Muslim are similar to those of a good Buddhist but the methods vary considerably. Like Buddhist Thai children, the young are instructed at home and in school but are required to attend the mosque regularly. The largest and most impressive mosque stands near Surin Bay in a largely Muslim agricultural area. Each Friday, the Muslims' sacred day, the dusty, public area in front of the mosque fills with stalls and vendors touting a varied selection of wares; the market comes to the locals once a week, saving them the long journey to town.

Elsewhere, such as on the eastern coast, are the smaller, less conspicuous mosques, immediately indentifiable by their half moon and star; if it were not for these symbols, the smiling faces that greet the visitor could just as easily be Buddhist ones. The sarong, used by the majority of Thai women, is worn by Muslims

Caged birds are a familiar sight in Phuket and, as in many parts of Asia, are kept for their melodious songs.
Muslim schoolgirls do not usually wear the traditionally head-covering in Phuket but the girls photographed left attend a strictly religious school and cover their hair in accordance with Koranic teaching. Dwarfed by sheer rocks on remote Phang Nga Bay, the small mosque of Ko Pannyi, far left, is the hub of activity for this Muslim village.

with a blouse so that, inkeeping with their customs, as much as is practically possible of a woman's body is kept covered. And when they attend the mosque they don a further shawl which entirely covers the head and shoulders, stretching down their backs. An element of purdah still exists at their more formal gatherings.

Although no Muslim festivals are singled out for public holidays, the Muslims in Phuket observe their month-long fast of Ramadan each year and enjoy the feasts and visits planned at the breaking of this month of culinary austerity.

Among the more puzzling anthropological questions is the origin of the *Chao Ley*, the Sea People or Gypsies, as they are frequently termed. These diverse people, often with strong, sturdy bodies and reddish tinges to their wavy hair, are believed to have come from Indonesia for they have peers in other parts of the world. In Phuket they have settled on Ko Sirey, Phi Phi Don and at Rawai beach. They speak their own

Twice a year the Chao Ley, or Sea Gypsies, celebrate an Animist festival to summon benevolent spirits at the beginning and end of the fishing season. An effigy, top far left, greets the community as they walk through an archway to their sacred ground. Here parcels of food are divided at a central area, below left, and prayers held to the Animist spirits. These seafaring people, left and below, lead simple lives and prefer to socialise within their own close-knit society.

language, utilising a variety of local words, and have their own practices. Largely Animist, an increasing number are beginning to adopt a recognised religion in answer to the government's campaign urging the *Chao Ley* to embrace a faith. Some are Buddhist believers and others have become Christian. In fact, Christian missionaries are now living in their midst and actively trying to improve their rather degenerate lifestyle. It is an exacting task for much of their self-respect has been eroded through alcoholism and social slighting. Despite the hardworking attempts, old habits die hard and their tribal ways will often take precedence, especially in the case of modern medicine.

The *Chao Ley* have survived the centuries as seafaring fishermen. They collected crabs and lobsters, fished the waters for a good catch and then began diving for pearls and oysters. Today they tend to fish less for commercial gain and dive more for their income. Since oysters (both for eating and for the pearl

A daily chore for Chao Ley women is prising open sharp-shelled oysters and cleaning them for sale. The shyness of this minority group shows in the naive, tentative girl photographed opposite.

The climax of the Loy Rua festival at Ko Sirey – the model boat, below right, is complete, above, and decorated with lighted candles, doll effigies, food and flowers, it floats out to sea at dead of night. Women and children watch the painstaking preparations and later join in the raucous fun and dancing which completes the festival.

industry) fetch a fair price and shell collecting is a profitable pastime, the *Chao Ley* make their living below water. Not without its problems. Weighted by a stone around the waist and fed by hose-piped air from the surface, divers plunge well beyond a safe depth and surface without sufficient decompression. The result? Life expectancy is not particularly high and some former divers are now incapacitated.

Twice a year, at the start and close of the fishing season (after the monsoons and before their onset the following year), the *Chao Ley* celebrate their *Loy Rua* festival with gay abandon. Building an effigy of a fishing boat and filling it with undesirable weapons — again models — it is taken out to sea as a peace offering to the spirits who hopefully, in turn, grant the *Chao Ley* a peaceful and harmonious life in the following season. All of this is accompanied by much merriment and quantities of potent Thai whisky.

Apart from the four major groups of inhabitants mentioned above, Phuket has attracted other minority settlers. These include the five Sikh families who moved from northern India to make their home in the island, the first of whom arrived some 50 years ago. They lead a quiet, fairly closely-knit life keeping to their own customs and earning a good living from textiles. Like other minority groups, they too have their own place of worship and a small, ochre-coloured Sikh temple stands unobstrusively on Montri Road.

Given Phuket's natural beauty, it is not surprising that a number of Caucasians have settled on the island. Some have chosen this spot for retirement, building their dream houses in what they consider a veritable Eden, while others are engaged in business activities and specifically, the tourist trade. As this industry has blossomed, their numbers too have increased, with the largest community settling in Patong valley. But the government is strict about requirements and notices admonishing would-be settlers are posted in conspicuous places. Over the last decade, Phuket and her developing industries have been kind to these immigrants and many have now married and settled permanently on this island which they have come to regard affectionately as their home.

Phuket Town

A century ago the capital of Phuket was a scruffy and relatively insignificant little village, far smaller than the town of Thalang in northern Phuket and of little importance to the island. With the expansion of tin mining last century in central Kathu District, labourers and their overlords started to settle in the southern regions and the town began to take shape.

It was a felicitious choice for the narrow river meandering through the settlement flowed out to sea in a sheltered, shallow bay — ideal for a small port. Old records mention how shallow draught boats used to sail up into the town, though it is hard to imagine such a sight when looking at what remains nowadays of the narrow, silty canal. But the port prospered as it provided an ideal outlet for ships carrying tin, while fishing — previously organised only on a small scale — began to gain commercial importance.

Today Phuket town is a bustling communications and administrative centre with a haphazard but comfortable blend of old and new, paralleling the development and economic fortunes of its citizens.

While the largely agrarian Thais preferred the rural areas of Thalang district and the Muslim Thais favoured the littoral, the Sino-Thais — businessmen for the most part, settled in Phuket town where, today, over 50,000 inhabitants are of Chinese origin.

It was under the Phuket governor Praja Rasada Korsimbi, in the first couple of decades of this century, that the modern town of Phuket — indeed, the island as a whole — began to blossom. Today he is still remembered with reverence by some of the town elders while his heirs have continued, in diverse ways, to make their mark on the evolution of Phuket.

Little remains of 19th century Phuket; building materials were usually natural ones, such as wood and palm thatch, which perished with the passage of time. In addition, there was a tendency among those early Chinese to demolish rather than to relocate when they wanted a more modern property. And most of what was not razed went up in a flaming inferno at the beginning of the century.

In its heyday Phuket town must have resembled Penang or Singapore with pastel-painted Straits Chinese terrace homes and shophouses lining the capital's booming streets. Like the houses, traditional forms of transport survive to this day and trishaw drivers, above, cluster outside the main market each morning waiting to deliver housewives and their provisions. Rain or shine, these sturdy cyclists are always poised for business.

Those streets in the heart of the capital named after neighbouring provinces to which they once led — Krabi, Phang Nga, Ranong — have few single-storey shop houses, complete with irregularly tiled roofs and attractively painted in those familiar pastel shades of dusky pink, peppermint green and egg shell blue, found throughout Chinese-inhabited Asia. The solid, double-storey shop houses, which might at first glance seem antiquated, are rarely older than 50 years for they are suffering, not from age, but neglect. Those intricate decorative details in balustrades, cornices and friezes that characterise Sino-Asian architecture are crumbling and, sadly, fading like a forgotten flower garden.

It is slightly different on the outskirts, where a number of imposing private houses, built in the Sino-Portuguese colonial style, evoke visions of the earlier era of prosperity. But some of those, too, merit a facelift which by now would probably be more structural than cosmetic. All these tangible reminders

of Phuket's history are in danger of disappearing.

In a town existing for over 100 years, it is difficult to find any structure that dates back more than a half century. But Government House, constructed over 70 years ago, has the distinction of being not only the oldest extant building but the first building in Thailand to be made out of concrete. With its 99 doors and two lone windows, it remains an impressive, airy structure reminiscent of colonial Cambodia. This likeness was not lost on the movie world who recently chose it to represent a Cambodian palace in "The Killing Fields".

Just across the tree-lined road stands the Provincial Court, a graceful, Portuguese-style colonial building. Under its elegant snowy-white cornice is inscribed the Thai date of its completion, 2459 or, in the Christian calendar, 1916. Thus these two civic buildings are said to be the oldest ones in town.

At the other end of the time scale, interspersed among the shop houses, are a few modern buildings,

The interior of Government House, below, now the civic centre of the island's administration, remains much as when it was first built in the second decade of this century. Another splendid old building, below left, has found new life as part of the Thai Airways property on Ranong Road.
Every Thai Buddhist home has a spirit house, above left, intended to ward off evil and adorned each day with gifts of food and flowers to appease malevolent spirits.

functionally simple in style and devoid of unnecessary decoration. The phase of modern architectural development dates from the time when Phuket town became a provincial capital and all those facilities expected of such a capital — hospitals, telecommunications buildings, banks, restaurants, hotels and travel agencies — reflect this latter-day expansion. One modern anomaly, however, is the Rasada Arcade. Small balconies, arches and dazzling white paintwork set aside this complex from its more mundane neighbours.

In the narrow backstreets of Phuket, road and pavement areas become extensions of homes and the locals live their lives as much out of doors as in. The street becomes a play area for children, a scene of neighbourly gossip for elders and an extended kitchen for women preparing family meals. Cane and straw weaving, right, are a familiar sight in Phuket's main shopping streets. These daily necessities for Phuketians – and inexpensive souvenirs for tourists – are woven in neighbouring Krabi and Phang Nga provinces.

Apart from its administrative role, Phuket town is the market and communications centre of the island. All provisions are dispersed here through the wholesalers and the fresh produce market. And, while there are numerous shops catering for all, it is the traditional market that is the pulse of the island.

From 5 a.m. until 11 a.m. daily this covered bazaar sells mounds of fresh fruit and vegetables, an exotic

หลี่หงวน

array of flowers, sides of raw, red meat, glistening piles of iced seafoods and a whole host of spicy mixes that form the basis of Thai cuisine. Here are the tiny turtles and frogs, the bound fowl and young chicks destined to be taken home for rearing or inclusion in the next family meal. To a cacophany of sound deafening the ears, an acrid whiff of strong spices wafts through the nose and leaves a lingering taste in the mouth while, through the dim light, one's eyes feast on the bustling sea of human activity. For the unaccustomed visitor it is a fascinating and somewhat exhausting excursion.

Outside the market on Rasada Street is Phuket's version of a central bus station. It is from this point that most of the island's blue and white wooden buses start their journey. Not for these tropical islanders the airtight, enclosed vehicles of northern Europe, but small, covered, open-air buses where passengers pack in like sardines, sitting facing each other in two rows. And there is always room for another. The alternative

Phuket Market is the social hub of the island for locals and the liveliest place to be in town early in the day. Stalls are piled high with fresh produce, cooked sweets and Thai delicacies, and the air filled with jarring fragrances like jasmine garlands, above left, mixed with tobacco for cheroot-like cigarettes, below far left.

public transport is by *tuk-tuk*, a motorised van that is hired on a first-come, first-served, sharing basis and which holds five or six passengers comfortably, or often too many more!

On the periphery of Phuket lie the industrial sectors — ramshackle buildings, scattered seemingly at random but forming the core of such necessary business. Here light industry and small workshops produce wooden goods, packaged food and bi-products of the fishing industry while sandwiched between these are the inevitable mechanical workshops for servicing the island's transport vehicles. Statistics state that one in two of the population owns a motor cycle, and the corner workshop where a grease-covered mechanic tinkers with a dissembled motor bike is a familiar sight.

Because of Phuket's administrative importance, urban hotels abound. While the lure of beach life entices tourists to the holiday hotels around the island's shore, the town hotels compensate with the glitter of

The old and the new cohabit in harmony in Phuket: despite their wealth Phuketians still refurbish old vehicles and often decorate them with gaudy panache. At the other end of the scale money can buy practically anything, including high fashion and modern-day amusements like roller skating at the local rink, advertised right.

พรศิลป์

KODAK

night life, a variety of top quality restaurants, more sophisticated service and full facilities for the businessman. There are four nightclubs — including three attached to the major hotels — which feature local and overseas singers, performers and guest revues, a number of cinemas (English language dialogue sets are available at a nominal extra charge) featuring local and western films, a large ten pin bowling alley and that curious Thai institution, the *ramwong*. There is something for everybody.

Every evening the four *ramwong* parlours open their doors at 9.00 and energetic males are invited to pay for a dance with a young hostess of their choice. Dressed in clothes more suited to a tennis court, these young girls dance to Thai or Chinese pop music for the small fee which goes to the *ramwong* manager. Strange though it may seem to western eyes, this system is very popular with Thais and, when a passing ship stops in Phuket, it is the favourite spot for the Thai crew who crowd the *ramwongs* beyond capacity for a few sweaty hours. On the stroke of 2.00, the parlours close their doors and the girls return to their dormitory accommodation. Many of these hostesses are aspiring actresses or dancers and regard this start as a first step towards their glittering goal.

The last spate of growth in Phuket began last decade. Tourism reached town. Between gold and jewellery shops, souvenir stores and hat sellers, are numerous town booking offices for resort hotels, travel agents, car rental agencies and the lucrative motor bike hire.

Yet all the expansion has done little to destroy the warm atmosphere of this small provincial town. Under the harsh and unforgiving midday sun, maybe it does not have the attraction of some other Thai towns but, bathed by the warm late-afternoon light, the tired buildings mellow in an unified tone, ugly overhead wires recede into the shadows and the town reflects the contentment of another day accomplished. And, unlike the inhabitants of some developing towns, the locals still have time to smile and greet passersby. Phuket is unhurried and not yet spoilt.

The ramwong, above left, is an old and very Thai tradition, something akin to dance halls of the Twenties and Thirties in the West. Here in Phuket the male chooses his partner and pays a very small fee for the privilege of one dance.
If the ramwong is too exotic for visitors, the alternative evening entertainment is more familiar bars, above and below left, which are well stocked with pretty Thai hostesses and lively entertainment that continues until the last customer calls it a night.

Taking the Plunge

Back in the early Sixties a few discerning travellers found the tropical climate and the unspoilt beauty of Phuket's beaches a magnetic lure. Those were the days before the advertisements enticing holidaymakers to Phuket became the norm; days when word-of-mouth was the only way Phuket was known in Europe. There were practically no resort hotels, Billy Budd's Patong cafe was open to backpackers and the young divers, surfers and sun worshippers generally had to make do with the most rudimentary accommodation.

But the crystal clear waters, prolific marine life and the many fine, safe, sandy beaches and coves soon became legendary and today, some 20 years later, they are enjoyed by the world's tourists. From late December to early March, the so-called dry season, Phuket is full of visitors. The between seasons, where scattered showers fall, and the monsoon season from June to September, are less popular and yet, since they have unpredictably sunny days, hotels still remain open.

The island's beaches lie exclusively on the west and southern seaboard, backed by the green hills and fringed by casuarinas, coconut and Borassus Palm. Towards the rocky promontories that separate the bays, the sandy seabed gives way to rocks and corals which support a varied system of marine life.

The eastern, flat coastal areas are fringed with mangrove swamp and the beaches, such as they are, totally unsuitable for resort life. Of the dozen or so beaches favoured by holiday-makers, no two are alike, each having its own endearing characteristics.

Today practically every beach can offer food and accommodation varying from the simple cabanas with their woven palm walls to the sturdier cottages in tropical, landscaped gardens, to the formal block-like hotels. Generally resort accommodation is constructed out of traditional local materials and provides adequate but basic facilities. And while the service is friendly, familiar and very willing, this air of informality is frowned upon in town hotels.

The first resort hotel to be constructed was Phuket Island Resort in 1973, on a rocky southern promontory,

Phuket's principle allure will always be its perfect beaches and translucent turquoise waters – sweeps of white coral sand lapped by gentle tropical seas. One of the island's archetypal bays is Nai Harn, above, which draws guests from hotels without their own beach.

Laem Ka. It commands a splendid view of the shallow, sheltered Chalong Bay to the south and overlooks the numerous rocky isles which form part of the Province.

From this initial littoral development, the metamorphosis of Phuket began. Slowly, and then with gathering speed, others followed suit.

At the beginning of the 20th century, four families trekked over the hills from Phuket and settled in Patong. Considered to be country hicks, not much thought was given to their rash move. Today they are among the most wealthy landowners in Phuket for it was Patong that was developed as the first beach resort, Patong that has the largest number of hotels and Patong that offers the best all round facilities demanded by a holidaymaker. Those four families owned something akin to a tourist goldmine.

The gentle, four kilometre curve of Patong is dotted with colourful umbrellas and deck chairs, while the calm sea is invariably enlivened with windsurfers,

Some say that sunsets on Kata Beach, left, are the most breathtaking in the world. An evening stroll on the beach, or a drink to the strains of classical music on the terrace of Club Mediterranée, is the perfect end to a day in the sun at Kata.
The warm waters of the Andaman Sea are rich in treasures like the drying corals, above left, and large lustrous pearls which are prized on the world market.
Overleaf: The rustic retreat of a Bangkok architect involved in several new luxury resort developments on Phuket – including design for Club Med's holiday village.

sailors and the occasional water scooter whipping up a wake as they pass by. It is a beach enjoyed by families and singles alike for, apart from the sports facilities available, an endless stream of itinerant hammock hawkers, sarong sellers, "gem" dealers, fruit vendors and cool drink purveyors parade like circus performers along the beach. One need hardly stir from the parasol except for the occasional refreshing dip in the Andaman Sea.

At night Patong comes alive with nightclubs and bars galore, where attractive Thai hostesses entice male passersby to stop for a drink or to linger even longer. The main street, populated by hired motor scooters, rented jeeps and window-shopping tourists, is a hive of activity. Seafood restaurants, local travel operators and souvenir sellers, offering their wares in an assortment of English, German and French, vie for a slice of the tourist trade. Like it or not, Patong is here to stay.

In the unlikely vicinity of the airport is a calm,

From brilliant blooms to brightly painted umbrellas, Phuket is a colourful blend of natural and man-made attractions cohabiting in visual harmony.

peaceful beach noted for its turtles and sea anemones. Nai Yang has now been declared a national park but it is still open to beach-loving visitors. The nearby beach of Mai Khao, which together with Nai Yang forms an 11 kilometre stretch of sand, is not suitable for swimmers as the steeply shelving shore creates rough, dumping waves and water currents.

One of the island's prettiest coves is Pansea, entirely surrounded by coconut plantations and featuring an attractive hillside hotel nestling in its centre. During the dry season snorkelling and swimming are safe, but come the rainy weather the sea is less predictable. Surin, its neighbouring beach, suffers similarly but remains a popular beach with locals during weekends. With the construction of a steep and outrageously scenic road between Surin and Patong, these two beaches are now accessible via the coast.

Phuket's preoccupation with tin mining has pushed the search offshore and in the centre of Kamala beach,

Resort life at Patong, Nai Harn, Kata and Rawai offers a full range of water sports and at Patong there's the added attraction of a pony trot down the beach in the evening breeze.

Overleaf: Tropical architecture nestling in its natural setting. The Pansea is a complex of nipa-thatch chalets overlooking the beach of the same name.

One of the delights of Thailand is the wonderful range of unusual tastes and nibbles on every roadside stall. In Phuket the wayside snacks move with the customer and a sidecar or stand selling soft drinks and fruit will materialise out of thin air.

an otherwise unspoilt stretch of coarse sand lined with feathery casuarinas, lies the ugly form of a tin dredger. Yet, despite this impairment, plans are afoot to develop the area.

Becoming increasingly popular are Karon and, to its south, Kata beaches (more or less linked to Patong by a new coastal road). Both have fine powdery white sand — so fine that it squeaks underfoot — and safe, seasonal swimming. While Karon offers a choice of cabana-style accommodation and a number of new cottage-style hotels, it is the new, yet unobtrusive, buildings of Club Mediterranée that command the splendid vistas of Kata beach.

What vision of Thai landscape could be more idyllic? As the steep, tree-clad hillside levels out to the peaceful paddy fields there is a subtle shift in verdant hue. The chartreuse young ears of rice contrast with the sombre mud-caked buffalos for whom home is the less poetic quagmires of Kata. Sea-ward a picturesque islet com-

The Utopia of city-bound visitors – warm blue seas, white sand and the ubiquitous curve of a palm tree. On the nearby Similan Islands, above right, few footsteps mark the powdery beaches and the world of Robinson Crusoe is at hand.
Overleaf: The smooth clear waters of Phang Nga Bay lure more adventurous travellers to explore a world of dramatic natural beauty.

pletes the sense of tranquillity as it shelters the bay from onshore winds. And, as if all of this were not sufficient, the renowed Kata sunsets add a grand *finale* to the days. Kata's calm waters are a haven for ocean-going yachts which seem to pose, as if bidden, nightly against the crimson skies of the setting sun.

Backed by a quiet stream, where kingfisher and heron preside over the peaceful waters and where wafts of wood smoke curl into the still air, lies the photogenic beach of Nai Harn. The backpacking hoards of the Seventies have moved on and in their wake a more respectable calibre of visitor has arrived. Like all the beaches, Nai Harn is served by frequent buses and minibuses from hotels in the vicinity which are not near a suitable beach for swimming.

At the south western extremity of Phuket island, standing sentinel to the southern seas, lies the rugged cape of Promthep. Nightly this grassy promontory, with its unusually stark palms, attracts visitors to watch the sun set over waters that once milled with pearl divers. To its north is Nai Harn and to its east lies the sheltered, somewhat silty shallow bays of Rawai and Chalong — both favoured by fishermen and, when the going is rough, yachtsmen. It is from here that a flotilla of small boats can be rented by the day or by the hour for exploring offshore islands. Although the shores of these two bays are not as enticing as those of the western beaches, many informal hotels dot the coastline and hillside offering tropical gardens and even a turquoise swimming pool, in one instance, as compensation for the poor beaches.

Every hotel and every travel agent is quick to point out the virtues of daily excursions to some of the islands. Phuket Province boasts 70 square kilometres of scattered islands in addition to the 564 sq. km. mainland. But it is to the neighbouring islands in Krabi and Phang Nga provinces that most visitors go.

The curious steep-cliffed rock formations of Phang Nga Bay — an aquatic landscape populated by stalactites and caves — rise perpendicular from the verdant green waters below. These limestone cliffs defy settlement except by a few birds. There is little noise, pollution or movement and to skim across the smooth waters is like slipping into an ethereal fantasy island.

Formed by the erosion of softer materials and then flooded in the semi-recent (10,000 B.C.) rise in sea level, Phang Nga Bay is attractive precisely for its primaeval beauty. A few fishing families dwell on the shore and even fewer on the islands which bear such names as "Puppy", "Nail" or "Leaning" island. Yet, as ancient cave paintings attest, even some 4,500 years ago Phang Nga was home to wandering fishermen.

Pannyi Island to the north of the bay has an ever-increasing stilted village lying in the shadow of a loaf-like rock formation. Some 2,000 Muslim fishing folk have made their homes above the shallow waters that teem with fish.

Further to the south, in Krabi Province, but still part of the same geological formation, lie the twin isles of Phi Phi Don and Phi Phi Ley. Discovered again by wandering fishermen, Muslim communities have settled on the former, while the vertical cliffs of the latter have prevented landing.

Much of Phang Nga Bay's fame comes from its association with James Bond – "A Man With A Golden Gun" was filmed here and visitors are taken to see "the real James Bond Island" by eager boatmen.
Idyllic Phi Phi Island, above left, can be seen from the air by southbound passengers – a spectacular haunt for divers in search of untouched coral reefs and crystal visibility.

For ocean-going yachtsmen, Phuket's tranquil waters provide a calm interlude and the chance to explore the splendours of surrounding islands. At Phang Nga Bay, right above and below, ancient wall paintings hide stories of the area's very early seafaring inhabitants.
Overleaf: At dawn the misty forms of Phang Nga's extraordinary limestone islands rise majestically above a glassy sea.

Phi Phi has become legendary among divers and fishermen for the corals have not been blasted by dynamite and the green waters — the waters in the bay formed by Phi Phi Don really are an indescribably deep-emerald green — support a healthy marine life. Here are the palm-fringed beaches, the translucent waters and powdery white sands yearned for by the sun-seeking hedonists of northern Europe. It is idyllic: a calm existence only interrupted at midday when pleasure boats bring the tourists for a seafood lunch at the island's only hotel. They depart, peace returns and the sun shines benevolently on the inviting shores.

The granite outcrops of the Similan Islands, some 50 nautical miles (95 km.) off Patong beach, are also beginning to feature as an excursion on some agents' books. The western shores of these low-lying islands are graced by dazzling white sands the consistency of talcum powder whose brilliance give the clear waters a variety of hue not often seen in Thailand. Like a flashing gem, the turquoise sea invites one to swim, wallow or dive beneath its glassy surface. Of the seven main islands, only one is inhabited — Island Four — and it is here that the Department of Nature Conservation has set up the beginnings of a village among virgin forest and verdant bush. It is still fairly rudimentary but they offer tents for hire at a minimal rate and, for those interested in wildlife, it provides an interesting and different environment.

A Thai cruise ship runs trips from time to time to both the Similans and Phi Phi, giving comfort-loving tourists the chance to see these slightly more remote spots which might otherwise remain rather inaccessible.

From Chalong and Rawai beaches small boats with outboard motors can be hired to visit the nearby islands. Among the favourites are Lone Island with sandy beach and fishing village, Mai Thon, a good spot for shell collectors and oyster hunters and the so-called Coral Island — Ko Hey — a popular spot for snorkellers and sun worshippers.

As long as developers realise that the charm of Phuket lies in its untampered natural beauty and in the crystal clear waters, unsullied by the effluent of shipping, the island will retain its international allure.

Sporting Chances

After a while even the indolent life of a lotus eater has its limitations and one's thoughts turn to something slightly more energetic. Phuket is fairly unique in being able to cater for all categories of visitors, sunbasking beach lovers and sports enthusiasts alike.

Long before the tourists were dipping their toes in the warm waters off Patong, keen divers were adjusting their tanks and plunging to the depths of the Andaman Sea. A couple of decades ago the marine life of Phuket was in pristine condition and despite recent dynamiting for fish, which has lead to inevitable degeneration, there is still much of interest, especially further away from favoured fishing grounds. Healthy hard and soft corals abound, consequently the chain of fish life is prolific. Add to this a clarity often exceeding 40 metres and the basics for superb diving are all present.

With the development of the tourist industry, the service systems required by diving enthusiasts have been established by a handful of competent companies. They supply all the gear and generally know the better dive spots. Clarity is taken for granted and dive talk naturally centres on the attractions.

Multicoloured fish that one normally finds in tropical aquariums are commonplace; sea ferns and intricate soft corals, whose underwater beauty is like a florist's shop in spring, tantalise the photographer and those larger creatures that thrill and sometimes evoke a shiver of fear are all present. From the dimunuitive Damsel fish, regally splendid Butterfly and Angel fish to the delicate but deadly Lion fish, Wrasse, Big Eye and Parrot fish and on up the scale to huge Garoupa, Manta and Eagle Ray. Then there are giant turtles, sharks — Nurse, Grey Reef, Leopard, White and Black Tipped — and the much maligned Moray Eel.

The best diving around Phuket is off the two Phi Phi islands and further afield in the Similans, where the relatively undamaged coral reefs support a varied and bountiful sub-aquatic community. The former has accommodation and facilities for air compression while the latter has only tented accommodation, no regular transport and no facilities. But that is far from a

From Phuket the keen sportsman and underwater enthusiast can sail or cruise to nearby Phi Phi or The Similans a little further afield. Here sophisticated resorts are replaced by tent living and the real rewards are to be found underwater.

There's no need to cruise offshore waters to see rich reef life: snorkellers spend hours of fascination over the coral off many Phuket beaches and enjoy visibility of around 25 metres in comfortably tepid seas.

deterrent, for the translucent waters of the Similans are a diver's dream. Among the popular dive spots are gently sloping coral reefs, huge subterranean architectural forms and the craggy outer reefs which plunge to Neptune's coffers. To add a further dimension to their already fascinating world, a couple of companies feature night dives where the powerful beam of a torch picks out somnolent shapes, immobile and at ease in their own world.

But the wonders of such scenarios are not the prerogative solely of divers. Snorkellers, too, can enjoy much of the same pageant in both the Similans and Phi Phi, as well as nearer home in Phuket. Off Phuket island there are a number of coral reefs accessible by a short swim from the beach which house a scintillating community of marine life. Those reefs just metres away from Kata, Karon and Patong are the most popular; clams, oysters, lobsters, starfish and sea cucumbers hug the rocks and coral seabed a few metres below the

Thailand

surface, while a kaleidoscope of fish — both large and small — populate the waters.

Masks, snorkels and fins are readily available for hire from hotels and private concessions on most of the popular beaches while some of the better dive shops offer a full range of modern equipment. Spear fishing is not yet outlawed, while the removal of live shells and coral is, and with good reason.

Above water the sail rules the waves. With a mountainous centre core which deflects air currents, Phuket is rarely without wind for long. During summer, offshore winds flatten the western waters making conditions ideal for dinghy, catamaran and board sailing. Patong and Kata are geared for such enthusiasts though the price of rental has been known to fluctuate with the strength of wind. Topcats and Hobiecats vie for the home reaches with Windsurfers and Mistrals, skimming across the glassy surface with fine precision.

In the past few years more yachts have sought

Anglers always talk about the "one that got away", but during Phuket's annual fishing tournament it's the one that's caught that counts. Marlin, tuna, sailfish and the occasional bonito are all permitted catches and tasty Spanish mackerel is always a favourite haul.

moorings in the sheltered bays of Patong, Nai Harn and Kata. In their wake has sprung up a lively yacht charter and sailing industry where one can sail to nearby islands for a day excursion or hoist canvas and breeze down to Malaysia's Langkawi or Penang islands for a five day trip. Some companies do all the hard work and some teach sailing skills on a learn-as-you-sail basis, but either way the coastal waters of southern Thailand are an idyllic location for cruising.

Water skiing enthusiasts have to contend with the very same winds that delight sailors though inevitably in the calmer, drier season in January and February, there are tranquil, windless days ideal for such pleasures. Water scooters, once a familiar sight on resort beaches, are beginning to disappear from Phuket because of unpleasant accidents and can only be found in a couple of places. It is probably for the best.

With the deep waters surrounding Phuket, conditions are ideal to game fish throughout the year. The an-

The Andaman Explorer, above, does as its name implies: on board this elegant schooner water sports enthusiasts can explore the remoter parts of Phuket, Phi Phi and the Similan Islands in comfort. Phuket's winds and waters are ideal for windsurfing, above right, and their rainbow sails dot the most popular resort bays. Water scooters, in contrast, are losing popularity but still provide moments of fun at Patong Beach.

YAMAHA

ภูเก็ต

nual game fishing tournament, just after Chinese New Year, attracts competitors from as far as Europe, North America and Australia. Lured by the thought of a "big one" — marlin, sail fish or barracuda — they take to the waters and patiently trawl with excellent chances of success providing they can stay the long fight. Tuna, Albacore and Spanish Mackerel provide the less ambitious angler with a gentler battle, while bottom fishermen can hook snapper or garoupa with ease.

Landlubbers have a variety of sporting options. Phuket town has a well-maintained private tennis club while visitors to the island have to content themselves with facilities offered by the better hotels. Golf, another Asian favourite, is available for locals and visitors alike at the Surin Golf Course, which squeezes in nine holes. But after the superbly manicured club lawns at Augusta or St. Andrews, the buffalo cut grass of Surin might appear a little rustic. Undaunted by such idiosyncracies, locals regularly fill the golf course once the sun has passed its zenith, and enjoy their play.

In Phuket town there is also a sports club — Siam Sports — offering gym facilities, aerobics and tables for badminton and snooker.

But for young Phuketians, as with youngsters all over the world, it is football that is the most popular all-round sport. Whether organised into teams or just a knock-about game with a local cane ball, it brings out an enthusiasm sometimes thwarted by the heat or humidity.

Other avid sportsmen love their game and work hard to keep up the standards. Fitness fanatics now enjoy a free fitness park on Rang Hill which has been installed for the health conscious. And very popular it is too! To the rhythmic beat of pop music, sports-clad citizens work out the prescribed programme at each point on a course. There is no excuse, for the exercises are clearly drawn and a recommended quota of repeats are given.

For the rest, sport is a spontaneous affair; a walk through the national parks or a family picnic, a swim off one of the more secluded beaches or an amicable game of volley-ball. Phuketians like being on the move and easily invent their own forms of entertainment.

Among the locals roller skating and golf hold sway as favourite sports. The young speed round a rink at the sports complex in Phuket Town while more sedate citizens tee off on a seaside course. Visitors can apply for temporary membership to the island's only club, but not with thoughts of other immaculate international courses in mind. This is golf Phuket-style.

Fresh Tastes

"Nai nam mee pla, Nai nar mee Kow" — "In the water there is fish, in the field there is rice", so wrote King Ramkhamkaeng in A.D. 1292. Nowhere in Thailand is this more true than in Phuket where the flat lands sway with the emerald green paddy and where seafood is one of the main attractions for visitors. The giant Phuket lobster is mentioned in revered tones by gourmands as far away as Bangkok and Singapore while the prawns (never call them shrimps), crustacea and fish are a talking point both around and away from the dining table. And rightly so, for such crystalline waters yield the freshest of seafood.

Thai cuisine had little publicity abroad until the development of the tourist industry in the last two decades. Nowadays Londoners, Berliners and New Yorkers can enjoy the same flavours and dishes as those served back home in Thailand. And for those who have never had the unique experience Thai food is often hot, fierier than Chinese Szechuan or Indian, and incorporates pungent ingredients such as lemon grass, *takrai*, tamarind, *makhaam* or kaffir lime, *bai makrood*, not used so frequently elsewhere in Asia.

Dotted around the villages, shores and towns of Phuket are hundreds of restaurants — many open air — from the most homely and rustic of eating houses to the smart hotel restaurants. Invariably the food is fresh, inexpensive and quite delicious.

Phuket's cuisine is essentially Thai, with Chinese and Malay additions to the largely sea produce, *Aahaan Taleh*, diet. Lobsters weighing around two kg. each, fat prawns, pomfret, mackerel, snapper and garoupa appear on all menus. Meat does not feature much, except in the more luxurious restaurants, and when it does it is, more often than not, buffalo.

If Bangkok's food is hot to the palate, then southern Thai dishes are an inferno. Those attractive, tiny chillis that creep into practically all recipes and are offered as an accompanying condiment in soya sauce, wreak havoc for those unaccustomed to this little "extra". Coupled with the fact that cooling coconut milk, a staple ingredient of northern food, is infrequently used

Phuket produces the staple of Asian cuisine – rice – and paddy fields are picturesque during the monsoon planting season of May to October when individual seedlings are plunged into the watery fields by hand.

there is little respite for the uninitiated. Luckily it is standard practice in Phuket to serve cool, weak tea and a range of iced beers or sodas as thirst quenchers.

As with their cousins to the north, two essential utensils feature in a Phuket kitchen. The first is a sturdy pestle and mortar, ideally made of granite for pounding, grinding and mixing, while the second is the traditional half spherical *wok* which serves as a multi-mode cooking pan. Fried, simmered or boiled, the *wok* manages it all over a small charcoal or gas fire. Thai food generally requires very little cooking so an adept chef can complete a dish from prepared ingredients in as little as two minutes.

Being a tropical island, Phuket is blessed with a proliferation of fresh fruit and vegetables which complement the Thai cuisine. Phuketians generally prefer to end a meal with fresh fruit rather than with sweet desserts which are kept for between-meals-snacks.

Many fruits are unfamiliar to western eyes but, once tasted, always remembered. Of the more familiar coconut, mandarin orange, pineapple, banana and papaya are abundant. Seasonally rambutan, jack fruit, durian, mangosteen, *lamut*, star fruit, water melon and guava also appear on the market.

Practically all cooks favour the superior fresh produce, including the various seasonings; in the rural areas they grow their own vegetables, *pak*, herbs and spices, exclusively for domestic use and rarely use dry produce. A mouthwatering aroma, attractively coloured and carefully garnished dishes are very important to Phuketians. Apart from the Thai standard such as Tom Yum Soup, fish, *pla*, curries, *kaeng*, or the spicy vegetable salads, *yam*, (which are of course laced with fresh chillis) found elsewhere in the Kingdom, Phuket has a couple of specialities of its own.

Noodles of all sizes regularly appear in Phuket fare, something that owes its inclusion to the Chinese and Malay settlers. But Phuket has evolved its own variety — Sapan noodles, named after the village of origin, which are something akin to Italian spaghetti.

Smoked, dried fish and shrimp are a firm favourite with locals. These are dried on bamboos over smouldering coconut husks to give them their characteristic flavour. The dried shrimps feature in a popular

Fresh produce and spices form the basis of most of the island's cuisine. The market, below left, sells all the ingredients including mounds of pungent, freshly-ground spice pastes. Below, a tray containing the main Thai ingredients for traditional dishes.

Phuket dish, smoked Shrimp Dip, where the shellfish are combined with other Thai staples — lemon grass, onions, garlic and chillis — in the ubiquitous pestle and mortar to form a blended mix. The same dried produce appears in other local adaptations of national dishes.

Perhaps not to everyone's taste, but certainly regarded as a delicacy in Phuket, is the sea grasshopper — or to give it its more prosaic name, sea lice! Found on the shores of a remote Phuket beach, this little creature is deep fried and served either as a starter or as an accompaniment to beer.

Snacks are as important to the Phuket diet as main meals. After a breakfast of rice porridge, curry or sticky rice, there comes a mild hunger gap which in many countries is satisfied by biscuits or cake. Phuket offers a range of "small eats" both savoury and sweet.

Through the streets of Phuket Town, and along the beaches of the island, the snack vendors hawk their wares. Naturally, fresh fruits are always available but in

Ban Rua restaurant, above and far left, on Kata Beach is famous for its exceptional sea food which the diner chooses and can then watch being cooked to his taste. Broiled lobsters, crabs and prawns are favourites with visitors and timber and thatch resort accomodation enhances the back-to-nature ambience.

addition they display such delicacies as dried coconut, local cashew and peanuts or dried squid. The latter, a popular snack, is toasted over charcoal and mangled to serve removing all moisture. Small meat kebabs, *satay*, and flattened, barbequed chicken are also prepared by specialist hawkers over portable charcoal burners. Small eats are big business in Phuket.

The Chinese have always loved their brightly coloured sweets while the Thais favour coconut and rice concoctions. Each morning in the market, and each afternoon on village streets, a range of multi-coloured cakes and sticky sweets are offered for as little as one baht each. Tapioca, coconut, palm sugar, peanuts, gelatin, pandan leaves, sticky rice and sugar combine to give a variety of nibbles, each of which is parcelled up in a piece of banana leaf and secured with a small matchlike stick. For many women these popular snacks provide a lucrative home industry.

On all the routes and beaches in Phuket there are stalls offering refreshing fruit drinks or natural coconut water – a delicious alternative. Grilled bananas are offered to hungry swimmers on Patong Beach while local housewives can pause to buy vegetables and fruit for the evening meal at wayside stalls like the one photographed left.

Glistening and shimmering in a variety of blue hues, these crabs and lobsters, above, are part of the day's catch at Po Bay on the north east of the island. Meals invariably centre around seafoods, right, and a mixture of Thai vegetables which can be fiery hot, or cool and soothing, accompaniments to the main dishes.

Overleaf: If fresh fruits don't excite the gourmet (and there are a variety of some 20 or more including the spiky durian photographed right, oranges, lychees and papaya) then Phuket's sweet nibbles deserve to be tried. These delectable desserts from palm sugar, rice, coconut, pandan and flour, can be a sticky stopgap in a long morning or afternoon.

Nature Wild and Tame

In the last few remaining pockets of primary jungle, like this scene in Khao Phra Thaeo National Park, Phuket's vegetation is dense and often so dark as to be almost impenetrable. Huge trees and tropical ferns soar metres above the ground while the soil is covered in a heavy layer of decaying humus providing an omnipresent, damp earthy smell.

Sometime just before dawn, prior to the first rays of sunlight touching the high tropical canopy, the jungle begins to awaken. Birds call, frogs croak, insects dry dew-covered wings and nocturnal creatures retire. It takes an hour of so for the sun to penetrate the thick vegetation and as it begins to climb to its zenith shafts of light spear the foliage and caress the half hidden fronds. The original forest still retains an air or primaeval majesty.

When the early voyagers visited Phuket they found vast tracts of primary jungle, "Marsh and mangrove, no very high mountains but several of moderate height." They related stories of rhino, tiger and wild elephant including a special white elephant. There were deer and wild boar in the hills and buffalo wallowing in mud holes on the coastal lowland.

Nowadays the visitor would be lucky to catch to glimpse of a mouse deer or flying lemur and the thick, leafy forest that once swathed 70 percent of the island, has been reduced to a mere 7·2 percent. Of this, half is now protected in the Khao Phra Thaeo National Park, a nature reserve created in 1978 to conserve indigenous vegetation, the Tone Sai Waterfall and local wildlife. Sadly the planting of rubber, the island's second economic mainstay for much of this century, is responsible for the destruction of the precious rain forest; a situation which is irrevocable.

Among the leafy greenery — ferns, palms, stately trees and the occasional flower — Phuket has a species of palm not found elsewhere. Named after the botanist who discovered its presence, the *Karedoxa Dolphin* now survives only in Phuket. Keen ornithologists also find a number of interesting birds although, with the devastation of the forest, their numbers have dwindled. The Crimson Sunbird, Scops Owl, Paradise Flycatcher and Red Jungle Fowl are all fairly easy to spot for a patient observer.

Around the same time the government decreed Khao Phra Thaeo a conservation area, it also decided to protect Nai Yang Beach where annually the giant Ridley Turtle lumbers ashore between October and

February to deposit its eggs in the sand. Too many turtles and eggs were ending up in the cooking pot and with the government's protection eggs are now carefully collected, hatched and reared under the auspices of the Aquarium, part of Phuket's Marine Biological Research Centre. Coincidentally with the Old Thai New Year on April 13, young turtles are released into the sea — being a symbol of longevity and good luck for Buddhists and Chinese, this ritual is seen as an auspicious start to the year.

Another sea creature in the same north western part of Phuket is the Sea Grasshopper. This curious crustaceous animal, the size of a small pebble, burrows down into the sands of Mai Khao beach where it thrives. Considered by many to be a delicacy, it too finds its way onto the dining table. Catching this lice-like creature is an exacting task for the experienced fisherman who watches for tell-tale bubbles in the sand in the wake of receding waves. He then thrusts down

Despite the dwindling wildlife, patient observers can be rewarded with the antics of chattering monkeys, or perhaps a glimpse of a Binturong peering through the thick foliage. In the dense undergrowth of Khao Phra Thaeo the rare and unique Dolphin Palm, below, spreads its fronds. And nearby the Tone Sai Waterfall attracts tourists and picknicking locals to its cool abode.

his rectangular net and scoops up all the sand in the probable area. Because it can take as long as one hour to find a kilo, the Sea Grasshopper is costly by the time it reaches the gourmet's plate. Nowadays few have the time or inclination to sift the sand in search of such a tidbit, and fewer menus offer this unique speciality.

There are remarkably few birds to be seen around the Phuket archipelago; excepting the occasional gull, Braminy Kite, Fish Eagle and the halcyon flash of a kingfisher, the skies are quiet. One feathered creature, however, does make a seasonal appearance with considerable consequences. Each year between January and April the Edible-Nest Swift returns to construct nests out of its own saliva in the limestone cliffs and caves of the area. Whilst its habits and nesting pattern are of interest, the great attraction is the nest for it forms the basis of the great Chinese delicacy, birds' nest soup — a tasty dish that is believed to have health-giving properties.

The Sea Grasshopper is a small, crustaceous creature, above far left, found almost exclusively on Mai Khao Beach just south of the airport. Catching them is a lengthy, taxing task since they burrow in the sand under breaking waves. A ranger, left, scooping up the delicacy for dinner with his homemade net device.
On the same littoral the Ridley Turtle, above left, lumbers ashore at night to lay its eggs in the warm sand during the early months of the dry season. And along freshwater streams the flashing wings of the kingfisher, above, are a familiar sight.

The season for collecting swiftlets' nests – the basis for birds' nest soup – starts around April in Phuket. Although there are caves full of such nests, the ones near Phi Phi Island, below, are particularly prolific. Once collected they have to be cleaned by hand to remove dirt and debris. Overleaf: splashes of brilliant lotus and waterlillies dot the surface of Thailand's ponds and canals while the tropical warmth keeps shrubs and trees blossoming year-round.

It takes an average of 15 days for the bird to construct a small nest in which it lays an egg, hatches and rears the fledgling. It then repeats the sequence in a second, adjoining nest until at the end of the season it has completed at least three nests. These are gathered by experienced collectors, while balancing precariously on a bamboo scaffolding high up in the caves. Phi Phi Ley, some 12 nautical miles from Phuket Island, is one of the areas favoured by the swiftlets and a Phuketian company has the exclusive right to collect and sell the nests. It is a time-consuming and tedious task to soften the fibres for cleaning and to remove every grain of dirt and a miscellany of feathers — but ultimately a worthwhile one. Their sales market now extends from Thailand to Singapore, Hong Kong and Europe.

On the flat, east coast of Phuket, the area of more sluggish tidal movement, lie the low mangrove swamps. Not as extensive as they used to be — mangrove trees make good fuel and wood props — the swamps support

a varied and interesting marine life. A walk around mangrove at low tide reveals brightly coloured crabs, feather-light insects and darting mud skippers.

The indigenous flora of Peninsular Malaysia naturally adapts itself with familiar ease to the climate of Phuket. The orchid, colourful logo of the national airline and so symbolic of the mysterious Orient to Westerners, thrives in Phuket and one orchid producer has achieved such success that he is able to export improved varieties to other Asian countries. Similarly those tropical and subtropical flowering trees and shrubs originally native to Africa and South America adapt easily to a new environment. Vibrant trees are a familiar sight in the suburbs while bougainvillea and frangipani are cultivated everywhere. Seasonally showers of golden Indian Laburnum, the dusky mauve of Jacaranda and the brilliant vermilion of the African Flame Tree burst through the otherwise verdant foliage and carpet the ground in bright patterns.

The Island's Riches

Rarely is a region blessed with the potential to develop two diametrically opposed, yet financially rewarding, industries. Phuket is one of those exceptions and for the last decade has been running two in tandem — though it now appears that tourism is poised to take the lead over tin mining.

Tin was discovered a couple of millenia ago in the Kathu district of Phuket and since then has been mined with varying degrees of seriousness, from the initial haphazard recovery by open-cast mining in the 17th century, to offshore dredging (introduced to the island in 1907) and recycling of placer deposits. Phuket's mineral recovery finally rose to an all time peak in early 1980 before the world slump in the tin market; the price fell and the permitted quotas declined. From the several hundred tons mined in the late 18th century, the figure rose to over 5,000 tons 100 years later, buoyed by the injection of Chinese business interests. In the early 1980's the figure began waning around the 3,500 metric ton mark and, unless world demand changes, it seems doomed to hover thereabouts.

Today some 2,400 people in Phuket are directly involved in tin mining while some 10,000 more are employed in ancilliary and support industries. Tin has been kind to the Phuketians, giving them a standard of living and an income far in excess of the national average. In fact, as a result of the province's tin deposits, which total some nine percent of the kingdom's annual production and nett over 100 million baht in royalties (the gross figure is around 1 billion baht) to the island, Phuketians enjoy the second highest per capita income in Thailand. A quick glance at the vehicles on the road and the comfortable, suburban houses soon confirms this.

Tin is never found alone. Mineral recovery in Phuket also yields tantalum (used in the aerospace industry), niobium and wolfram, all of which are important to Phuket, fetching some 150 million baht annually, while deposits of uranium, diamonds and gold are not in sufficient quantities to be considered viable. Despite the higher value of the latter minerals and metals, tin

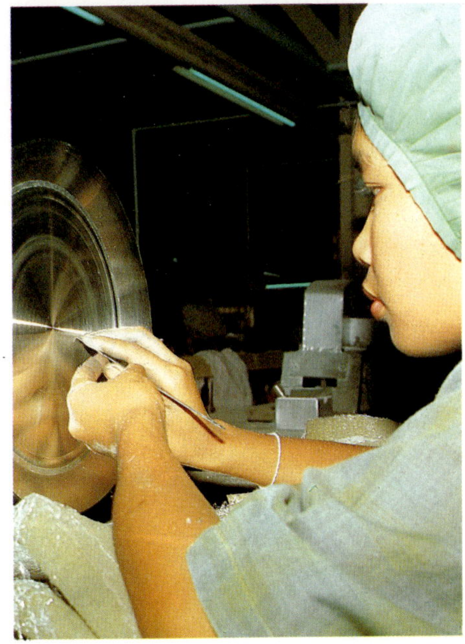

Since the first tin dredger was introduced to Phuket in 1907 they have become an intrinsic part of the landscape – a reminder of the natural resource that first brought wealth to the island's people in the 19th century. Pewterware is fashioned from Phuket tin at Siam Pewter Company in Bangkok, above, and then sent back to the island's shops.

Despite the increase in tourist-related industries, commercial fishing still thrives: the locals catch for their own needs using timeless methods in both salt and fresh water while the "big boys" of the business set to sea in trawlers. Every morning glistening catches of fresh fish are heaped on slabs in the town's main market, below right.

still remains the most important commodity.

Previously all tin was sent to Penang to be smelted but since Thaisarco built its smelter in Makham Bay, the majority of the ore is now processed on the island. A small amount is reserved, however, for another industry — pewter. Phuket used to produce its own pewter goods from local tin, (with the three percent addition of antimony and copper) but found that it was easier to operate a factory in Bangkok. Siam Pewter Company, employing some 65 people in the capital, now fashions quality pewterware exclusively out of Phuket tin and returns a selection of its items to the island for sale.

Fishing is an important source of revenue to Phuket. It is estimated that there are some 350 industrially operated fishing boats owned by a number of private companies whose fleets trawl the waters of southern Thailand. These employ some 10,000 local fishermen, added to which are a fair number of small community

Rubber changed the physiognomy of Phuket some 80 years ago and now one sees rubber plantations, with their familiar clay cups catching liquid rubber, above, everywhere on the island. The trays of firm rubber are mangled into rectangles, above right, and then strung out to dry like laundry in the sun.

fishing folk who generally supply local needs. Top of the commercial catch list are sardines and mackerel, much of which is frozen for export whilst the balance is processed into fish pastes and sauces, fish fertilisers and animal feed. The annual yield fluctuates from year to year but averages around 150 million baht.

At the turn of the 20th century the landscape of Phuket was largely virgin, except for the few gaping scars of tin mining operations. It was not to last. In 1903 the first rubber plants were introduced from Malaysia and Singapore and the stately forests began to diminish. Today, 70 percent of the agricultural plantations are under rubber, a total of some 16,000 hectares or 29 percent of Phuket island, with the largest concentration in rural Thalang district.

Like tin, the world requirement for rubber has declined but Phuket has managed to maintain its production with an annual revenue of around 1,100 million baht. While there are a number of huge rubber estates contributing to this annual output, 80 percent of the trees belong to smallholders whose land can vary from one to four hectare. And, with such a plot, it can be a comfortable life for the hard worker.

Extraction of rubber is the same whether for estate owner or smallholder. In the early hours of each morning a slanting incision is made around one third of the tree bole's circumference and the white, rising sap trickles slowly into a small cup ready for collection some seven hours later. This white liquid is emptied into trays where it congeals into latex and is then mangled into rectangles resembling white car mats. After a short drying time the mats are sold to a central rubber dealer and the planter's job is complete.

The rubber plant has no commercial value for its first years and while the rows of spindly trees grow, farmers usually plant a secondary cash crop such as tapioca or pineapples in between. Phuket pineapples are deliciously sweet and bear fruit twice a year. Thus the demand for this fruit has increased considerably and a number of smallholders have converted their land exclusively for this popular fruit.

Other commercially grown agricultural products on the island include cacao, mangosteens, cashew nuts, durians and vegetables. In some of the quieter valleys

market gardens exist supplying produce for local consumption. Rice, found throughout the lower reaches of Phuket and covering some 2,000 hectares, is seasonal with an average of two annual crops. Palm oil, too, has been introduced to Phuket and is now grown near Tha Rua in one single hectare block. The palm nuts are sent to Krabi province for processing.

For centuries the fishermen of Phuket have found pearls on the seabed, but it is only during the last two decades that they have been farmed commercially. Privately owned Naga Pearls produces some 4,000 pearls per annum; not, however, the small pea-sized ones but pearls usually in excess of 15 millimetres which can fetch as much as 100,000 baht each on the world market.

To culture these pearls, the company buys young oysters of the *Pinctada maxima* variety from local divers and other sources which, after a period of recuperation, are opened and a nucleus stone intro-

The small but relatively profitable palm oil industry has its processing plant in Krabi Province but the handsome trees, far left, can be seen growing near Tha Rua crossroads. The russet palm oil kernels, above, are gathered and crushed to extract the universally useful oil. Cacao is a relatively new crop for Phuket: once a year the ripe pods, left, are gathered and the separated seeds sent for processing by the island's chocolate industry.

duced. As a natural protection from this intruder, the oyster secretes the highly prized calcium deposit which coats the immature pearl. The average Naga pearl takes two years to grow and the oyster requires turning every few weeks to ensure the pearl's even coating. The majority of the reclaimed pearls are then exported while a few only are retained for local sale.

Another marine-related industry has grown up around Phuket's varied and superb seashells. Once found only in the fishing nets that trawled to depths of 300 metres, these beautiful objects are now actively sought by divers. Phuket has one of the world's finest ranges of tropical shells and when cleaned, polished and fashioned into belts, lamps or ornaments, these make an attractive souvenir industry. Such has been the demand for Phuket's seashells that one company now exports over 50 percent of its production to department stores in the United States.

The last, most recent, and most profitable, industry

Corals and shells, above and right, are offered by the sea for thriving industries. But the shells that are most precious are **Pinctada maxima** *– a variety of oyster that nurtures implanted stones and turns them into highly prized pearls of thumbnail size. Implanting the nucleus, above right, is a delicate operation and for two years the oyster shells are nurtured at Naga Pearls, far right, before their lustrous product can be harvested.*

is tourism — a business into which many of the tin and rubber barons are beginning to invest their money. From 1,000 annual visitors in the late 1960's, Phuket today welcomes over 300,000 tourists a year, many of whom arrive by the frequent international flights and spend around 1·5 billion baht as a result of their stay. The demand for accommodation and facilities has radically changed the littoral face of the island and yet has done little to spoil its intrinsic charm.

In a decade the number of available rooms has risen from a few score to over 4,200 and the infrastructure required to serve this influx modified accordingly. Tourists can now enjoy architect-designed hotels whose facilities are of an international standard as well as less formal, cabana-style accommodation. As each year passes more and more of the fine sandy shores, so beloved by sun worshippers, boast new hotels, accommodation and restaurants. In two short years tourism has boomed to become number one baht earner.

Practical Information

Access

By Air:

There are over 30 international airlines serving the capital of Thailand and from there passengers can fly to Phuket by the frequent services offered by Thai Airways International as well as daily flights on the domestic airline, Thai Airways. In addition, Thai Airways International operates direct flights from Singapore and Malaysia: its Royal Orchid holidays feature an inclusive package to Phuket, including transfers, accommodation, flights and some meals. All flights from and to Bangkok take approximately 70 minutes.

Phuket International Airport is served by Thai Airways buses, taxis and *tuk-tuk* which link the town with the airport some 32 km. away.

By Land:

There are a number of private bus companies operating frequent services to and from Bangkok with a choice of air-conditioned (approx. nine departures daily) and non-airconditioned (approx. seven departures) coaches — the factor which dictates the ticket price. The journey takes approximately 14 hours and buses leave from Phang Nga Road.

Buses also connect southbound to Singapore via Hat Yai and Butterworth, as well as to all major cities in southern Thailand.

There is no direct train connection between Bangkok and Phuket. Trains travel to Surat Thani from Bangkok and from this eastern seaboard town there are numerous bus and taxi connections. The total journey takes around 14 hours.

Climate

The island enjoys warm to hot weather throughout the year. Temperatures rarely fall below 25°c or rise above 33°c. The monsoon season begins around June and continues until October, with a sporadic showery season either side. During the monsoon it rains frequently and heavily with periods of clear weather in between. The "dry" season is from January to March when it is unlikely to rain severely.

Currency

The Thai currency is known as the baht; coins of one and five baht are in circulation whilst notes start with ten, 20, 100 and 500 baht.

Entry Formalities

For most visitors planning to stay less than 14 days, and possessing an onward airline ticket, a visa is not necessary. Overseas Thai Consulates and Embassies can further advise on requirements for those in doubt and also issue a visa for visitors planning a longer stay.

What to See

Phang Nga Bay, with its extraordinary rock formation; Wat Chalong and Wat Pratong; the Aquarium; Phuket Market; Tone Sai Waterfall; Phi Phi Is-

Phang Nga Province
Sarasin Bridge
Mai Khao Beach
View Point
Ko Lawa
Airport
Phang Nga Bay
Nai Yang Beach
MUANG MAI
Ko Naka
Po Bay
Wat Pratong
Ko Naka Noi
THALANG
Tone Sai Waterfall
Bang Thao Beach
Heroines Monument
Pansea
Surin
Ko Rang Yai
Wat Tha Rua
Kamala
Ko Ma Prao
SAPAN
Waterfall
KATHU
Rang Hill Viewpoint
Ko Siray
PATONG
Patong Bay
Bang Po Dam
PHUKET
Gypsy Village
PHUKET
Andaman Sea
Wat Chalong
Karon Bay
Makham Bay
Kata
Chalong Bay
Aquarium
Lone Island (Ko Lone)
Ko Mai Thon
Nai Harn
Rawai Beach
Promthep Cape
Phi Phi Don
Ko Kaew Yai
Ko Hey
Ko Kaew Noi
Phi Phi Ley

land excursions; Sea Gypsies; a pearl farm; the view points at Rang Hill, Promthep Cape and above Kamala Bay.

Hotels

In Phuket town:

*Pearl Hotel,
Montri Road.
Phone: 211901

*Phuket Merlin,
158 Yaowaraj Road.
Phone: 212866

Thavorn,
74 Rasada Road.
Phone: 211333

Imperial,
Phuket Road.
Phone: 212311

Montri,
Montri Road.
Phone: 212936

Budget Hotels:

On On,
Phang Nga Road.
Phone: 211154

Rama,
231 Yaowaraj Road.
Phone: 211867

Resorts

Patong

*Patong Merlin,
Phone: 321070-4

Club Andaman,
Phone: 321102

Patong Beach Hotel,
Phone: 211426

*Coral Beach Hotel,
Phone: 321106-15

*Phuket Cabana,
Phone: 321138-40

Patong Villa,
Phone: 321132-3

Seagull Cottage,
Phone: 321238-43

Thara Patong,
Phone: 321520

Patong Bay Garden Resort

Kata Beach

*Club Mediterranée,
Phone: 211901-4

Kata Inn,
Phone: 212901 Ext 072

Kata Villas,
Phone: 211274

Kata Noi

Kata Thani,
Phone: 212901-4

Rawai

*Rawai Resort,
Phone: 212943

Laem Ka

*Phuket Island Resort,
Phone: 215950-5

Nai Harn

Phuket Yacht Club,
Phone: 211274

Karon Beach

*Karon Villa,
Phone: 212709, 216574

Karon on Sea

Karon Inn

Pansea

*The Pansea,
Phone: 212901-4

Lone Island (Ko Lone)

Lone Island Resort,
Phone: 212526

A whole range of budget accommodation exists on most of the beaches while Nai Yang has basic accommodation offered by the Department of Wildlife.

* With swimming pool.

Restaurants:

Where specified, S = Seafood, C = Chinese, T = Thai

Phuket

S Laem Thong, Montri Road, Phone: 211269

C Rooftop, Pearl Hotel, Phone: 211044

C Tien Kong, Phuket Merlin, Phone: 212866

C Lai An, Rasada Road. Phone: 211245

Jap Tunka Cafe,
TC Rang Hill, Kosimbee Road. Phone: 211500

T Pajit Thai Food, Phang Nga Road.

T Maeporn, Phang Nga Road. Phone: 212106

Prom Jai, Rasada Road. Phone: 212892

Resorts

S Kan Eng II, entrance to Chalong Bay Bungalow, Chalong. Phone: 216288

S Ko Sirey, Sirey Island

S Wang Pla I, Sirey Island

S Plaplao Rawai, Rawai Rimlay, Rawai

TS Boat House, Kata Beach

TS Patong Seafood, Patong

S Loma, Patong

Other informal restaurants, too numerous to mention, can be found on every beach around the island.

Useful Addresses

For up-to-date information on Phuket and accommodation: Tourism Authority of Thailand (T.A.T.) and Tourist Police, 73–5 Phuket Road, Phuket. Phone: 212213, 211036

Hospitals

(Western-trained and English-speaking staff are available)
Mission Hospital, Thepkasatri Road. Phone: 212386

Phuket Ruamphaet Hospital, Phuket Road. Phone: 211578

Money changers

The Siam Commercial Bank, Rasada Road. Phone: 212254-5

The Thai Farmers Bank, Phang Nga Road. Phone: 212061 (also on Patong Beach)

The Asia Trust Bank, Rasada Road. Phone: 212397 (also located at the airport)

The Bangkok Bank, Phang Nga Road. Phone: 211294-5

Pearl Hotel, Montri Road.
Phone: 211044

Phuket Merlin Hotel,
Yaowaraj Road. Phone: 212866

Phuket Island Resort, Laem Ka.
Phone: 212910, 215950-5

(Some 10 other banks also exist throughout town)

Night Food Markets:
Imperial, opposite Imperial Hotel, Phuket Road.
Nimit, Tilokutis Road.

Telecommunications:
Post Offices on Montri and Bangkok Roads.
Telephone services from Telephone Centre on Phang Nga Road.

Night Clubs:
Marina, Phuket Merlin Hotel.
Phone: 212866

The Wave, Pearl Hotel.
Phone: 211044

Hong Thong, Phuket Road (by Paradise Cinema).
Phone: 211642

Churches:
Catholic, Soi Talingchan.

Seventh Day Adventist, Thepkasatri Road.

Takreng Church, Chao Fah Road.

Mosques:
Soi Talingchan
(All the above are located in Phuket town).

Airlines:
Thai Airways International, Montri Road (opp. Pearl Hotel), Phuket
Phone: 212400

Thai Airways, Ranong Road, Phuket
Phone: 211195

Additional Information

Travel Agents:

Bhuket Travel n' Tour,
Rasada Road. Phone: 212040

Lone Island Tour,
Rasada Road. Phone: 212526

Phuket Centre Tour,
Rasada Road. Phone: 212892

Phuket Horizon Tour,
Rasada Road. Phone: 211151

Sun and Sand Tour,
Pearl Hotel. Phone: 211044

Sunshine Tours,
Phuket Road. Phone: 212889

Montri Tour,
Montri Hotel. Phone: 212936

Phuket Island Tour,
Rasada Road. Phone: 211421

Sports Facilities:

Diving
Fantasea,
61/12 Patong Beach;
Phuket, P.O. Box 74
Phone: 321309
Telex: 69513 SHPSERV.
Scuba diving trips,
living on a fully-serviced yacht.
Phi Phi and Similan Isles;
night and day dives.

Phuket Aquatic Safaris
Rasada Centre,
Rasada Road,
Phuket, P.O. Box 94.
Phone: 216556.
Scuba diving trips to
Similans and Phi Phi.

Santana, P.O. Box 79,
Patong Beach.
Diving and sailing trips
to Phi Phi.

Siam Diving and Sports,
P.O. Box 58,
Phuket, Telex: 65517.
Diving trips in and around
Phuket, Phi Phi and the
Similans.

General

Siam Sports Club,
171 Yaowaraj Road,
Phuket. Phone: 212851

Fishing
Southern Marine Co.,
Rasada Centre,
Rasada Road,
Phuket.
Deep sea fishing trips
and fishing and diving
equipment for hire.

Car Hire
Pure Car Rental,
Rasada Road,
Phuket.
Phone: 211002.

Festivals:

The dates of many vary from year to year. Here is an approximate guide:

February 4, Maka Puja
February, Chinese New Year (three–ten days)
April 13, Songkran or Water Festival
September/October, Vegetarian Festival (10 days)
November 7, Loy Krathong
December 31, New Year's Eve
June and November, Loy Rua Gypsy Festival

Photography and text by
Fiona Nichols
Printed in Singapore
September 1985
Publisher's number: 280

Additional photography: page 28 bottom, and page 127 left, Kraipit Phanvut; this page, Dallas Heaton/The Stock House. Historical map on page 5, courtesy of Antiques of the Orient, Singapore. Contemporary map on page 123 by Wendy Moore.